MW01288729

EASY INDONESIAN COOKBOOK

THE EFFORTLESS CHEF SERIES

VOL. #XIV

By
Chef Maggie Chow
Copyright © 2015 by Saxonberg
Associates

Published by
BookSumo, a division of Saxonberg
Associates
http://www.booksumo.com/

A GIFT FROM ME TO YOU...

I know you like cultural food. But what about Japanese Sushi?

Join my private mailing list of readers and get a copy of *Infinite Sushi: A*

Complete Set of Sushi and Japanese Recipes by fellow BookSumo author Hashimoto Kazuma for FREE!

Sign Me Up!

Enjoy some of the best sushi available!

You will also receive updates about all my new books when they are free. So please show your support.

Also don't forget to like and subscribe on the social networks. I love meeting my readers. Links to all my profiles are below so please click and connect :)

Facebook

Twitter

INTRODUCTION

Welcome to *The Effortless Chef Series*!
Thank you for taking the time to
download the *Easy Indonesian
Cookbook*. Come take a journey with me
into the delights of easy cooking. The
point of this cookbook and all my
cookbooks is to exemplify the effortless
nature of cooking simply.

In this book we focus on the Country of
Indonesia. You will find that even
though the recipes are simple, the taste
of the dishes is quite amazing.

So will you join me in an adventure of
simple cooking? If the answer is yes
(and I hope it is) please consult the table
of contents to find the dishes you are
most interested in. Once you are ready
jump right in and start cooking.

— Chef Maggie Chow

TABLE OF CONTENTS

LEGAL NOTES

Chapter 1: Easy Indonesian Recipes

Indonesian Classical Satay

Ingredients

- 3 tbsps soy sauce
- 3 tbsps tomato sauce
- 1 tbsp peanut oil
- 2 cloves garlic, peeled and minced
- 1 pinch ground black pepper
- 1 pinch ground cumin
- 6 skinless, boneless chicken breast halves - cubed
- 1 tbsp vegetable oil
- 1/4 cup minced onion
- 1 clove garlic, peeled and minced
- 1 cup water
- 1/2 cup chunky peanut butter
- 2 tbsps soy sauce
- 2 tbsps white sugar

- 1 tbsp lemon juice

skewers

Directions

- At first you need to set a grill or grilling plate to high heat and put some oil before starting anything else.
- Coat chicken with a mixture of soy sauce, cumin, tomato sauce, black pepper, peanut oil and garlic, and refrigerate it for at least 15 minutes.
- Cook onion and garlic in hot oil until brown before adding water, sugar, peanut butter and soy sauce into it.
- Add lemon juice after removing from heat.
- Thread all the chicken pieces into skewers
- Cook this on the preheated grill for about 5 minutes each side or until tender.
- Serve this with peanut sauce.

NOTE: If using a grilling plate please adjust the cooking time of the meat, to make sure that everything is cooked fully through.

NOTE: For peanut sauce recipe please see recipe for <u>Satay Ayam</u>.

NOTE: You will find that a few of these recipes call for a grill. Real Southeast Asian food is cooked street-style over an open flame, outside. For maximum authenticity use a grill.

Serving: 6

Timing Information:

Preparation	Cooking	Total Time
25 mins	20 mins	1 hr

Nutritional Information:

Calories	329 kcal
Carbohydrates	11.8 g
Cholesterol	67 mg
Fat	18.2 g
Fiber	2.2 g
Protein	30.8 g
Sodium	957 mg

* Percent Daily Values are based on a 2,000 calorie diet.

PORK SATAY

Ingredients

- 2 cloves garlic
- 1/2 cup chopped green onions
- 1 tbsp chopped fresh ginger root
- 1 cup roasted, salted Spanish peanuts
- 2 tbsps lemon juice
- 2 tbsps honey
- 1/2 cup soy sauce
- 2 tsps crushed coriander seed
- 1 tsp red pepper flakes
- 1/2 cup chicken broth
- 1/2 cup melted butter
- 1 1/2 pounds pork tenderloin, cut into 1 inch cubes
- skewers

Directions

- At first you need to set a grill or grilling plate to medium heat and put some oil before starting anything else.

- Blend garlic, ginger, soy sauce, peanuts, lemon juice, honey, green onions, coriander, and red pepper flakes in a blender until you see that a smoothness is achieved.
- Coat pork cubes with this mixture by placing everything in a plastic bag and refrigerating for at least six hours.
- Thread pork cubes taken out from the bag onto skewers and boil the remaining marinade for about 5 minutes
- Cook this on the preheated grill for about 15 minutes each side or until tender, while brushing frequently with the cooked marinade.
- Serve with the remaining marinade.

NOTE: If using a grilling plate please adjust the cooking time of the meat, to make sure that everything is cooked fully through.

Serving: 4

Timing Information:

Preparation	Cooking	Total Time
30 mins	10 mins	6 hr 40 mins

Nutritional Information:

Calories	683 kcal
Carbohydrates	22.1 g
Cholesterol	156 mg
Fat	49.7 g
Fiber	4.2 g
Protein	41.6 g
Sodium	2332 mg

* Percent Daily Values are based on a 2,000 calorie diet.

Indo-Chinese Spiced Rice

Ingredients

- 3 tbsps vegetable oil
- 1 large onion, chopped
- 2 jalapeno peppers, seeded and minced
- 2 cloves garlic, crushed
- 1 tsp ground turmeric
- 1/2 tsp ground cinnamon
- 2 cups uncooked long-grain white rice
- 2 (14.5 ounce) cans chicken broth
- 1 cup water
- 1 bay leaf
- 2 green onions, chopped

Directions

- Cook onion, garlic and jalapeno peppers for about eight minutes before adding turmeric and cooking for two more minutes.
- Now add chicken broth, bay leaf and water, and cook all this for

about 20 minutes after bringing
this mixture to boil.

- Turn the heat off and let it stand
  as it is for about five minutes.
- Sprinkle some green onion over it
  before serving.

Serving: 8

Timing Information:

Preparation	Cooking	Total Time
10 mins	25 mins	35 mins

Nutritional Information:

Calories	226 kcal
Carbohydrates	39.8 g
Cholesterol	0 mg
Fat	5.5 g
Fiber	1.3 g
Protein	3.7 g
Sodium	4 mg

* Percent Daily Values are based on a 2,000 calorie diet.

Nasi Goreng

(Chicken Fried Rice Dish with Sauce)

Ingredients

- 12 ounces long grain white rice
- 3 cups water
- salt to taste
- 2 tbsps sunflower seed oil
- 1 pound skinless, boneless chicken breast halves
- 2 cloves garlic, coarsely chopped
- 1 fresh red chile pepper, seeded and chopped
- 1 tbsp curry paste
- 1 bunch green onions, thinly sliced
- 2 tbsps soy sauce, or more to taste
- 1 tsp sunflower seed oil
- 2 eggs
- 2 ounces roasted peanuts, coarsely chopped

- 1/4 cup chopped fresh cilantro

Directions

- Bring a mixture of rice, water and salt to boil in a pan before turning down the heat to low and cooking for another 25 minutes to get the rice tender.
- Cook chicken, garlic and red chili pepper for about seven minutes before adding curry paste, cooked rice and green onion into it and cooking for another five minutes, while adding soy sauce at the end.
- Put the rice mixture aside; cook egg in the in a pot and when finished, mix it with the rice very thoroughly.
- Garnish with peanuts and cilantro before serving.

Serving: 6

Timing Information:

Preparation	Cooking	Total Time
15 mins	35 mins	50 mins

Nutritional Information:

Calories	430 kcal
Carbohydrates	51.5 g
Cholesterol	101 mg
Fat	13.8 g
Fiber	2.7 g
Protein	24.3 g
Sodium	491 mg

* Percent Daily Values are based on a 2,000 calorie diet.

INDONESIAN INSPIRED KETCHUP

Ingredients

- 1 1/4 cups soy sauce
- 1 cup molasses (such as Grandma's®)
- 2 tbsps brown sugar
- 1 cube chicken bouillon (such as Knorr®)

Directions

- Mix all the ingredients mentioned above in a saucepan and cook it over low heat until you see that a slow boil is reached.
- Turn the heat off and cool it down.
- Store this in an airtight container and in a refrigerator.

Serving: 3

Timing Information:

Preparation	Cooking	Total Time
5 mins	15 mins	20 mins

Nutritional Information:

Calories	31 kcal
Carbohydrates	7.4 g
Cholesterol	< 1 mg
Fat	0 g
Fiber	0.1 g
Protein	0.5 g
Sodium	479 mg

* Percent Daily Values are based on a 2,000 calorie diet.

INDONESIAN FRIED RICE

Ingredients

- 1/2 cup uncooked long grain white rice
- 1 cup water
- 2 tsps sesame oil
- 1 small onion, chopped
- 2 cloves garlic, minced
- 1 green chile pepper, chopped
- 1 small carrot, sliced
- 1 stalk celery, sliced
- 2 tbsps kecap manis
- 2 tbsps tomato sauce
- 2 tbsps soy sauce
- 1/4 cucumber, sliced
- 4 eggs

Directions

- Bring a mixture of rice and water to boil before turning down the heat to low and cooking for 20 minutes.

- Cook onion, green chili and garlic in hot oil for a few minutes before adding carrot, rice, tomato sauce, celery, soy sauce and kecap manis, and cooking for another few minutes.
- Transfer this to a bowl, while garnishing with cucumber slices.
- Cook eggs in the pan and when done, put them over rice and vegetables.

Serving: 4

Timing Information:

Preparation	Cooking	Total Time
25 mins	15 mins	40 mins

Nutritional Information:

Calories	215 kcal
Carbohydrates	26.7 g
Cholesterol	186 mg
Fat	7.7 g
Fiber	1.6 g
Protein	10 g
Sodium	1033 mg

* Percent Daily Values are based on a 2,000 calorie diet.

INDO-CHINESE CHICKEN

Ingredients

- 1 cup uncooked long grain white rice
- 2 cups water
- 1 pound fresh green beans, trimmed and snapped
- 2 tsps olive oil
- 1 pound skinless, boneless chicken breast halves - cut into chunks
- 3/4 cup low-sodium chicken broth
- 1/3 cup smooth peanut butter
- 2 tsps honey
- 1 tbsp low sodium soy sauce
- 1 tsp red chile paste
- 2 tbsps lemon juice
- 3 green onions, thinly sliced
- 2 tbsps chopped peanuts(optional)

Directions

- Bring a mixture of rice and water to boil before turning down the heat to low and cooking for 20 minutes.
- Put green beans in a steamer basket over boiling water and steam it for about ten minutes or until you find that it is tender.
- Cook chicken in hot oil for about five minutes on each side.
- Combine chicken broth, honey, soy sauce, peanut butter, chile paste and lemon juice in a pan, and cook it for about five minutes before adding green beans.
- Serve this over rice and garnish with green onions and peanuts.

Serving: 4

Timing Information:

Preparation	Cooking	Total Time
15 mins	30 mins	45 mins

Nutritional Information:

Calories	530 kcal
Carbohydrates	58.1 g
Cholesterol	59 mg
Fat	18.6 g
Fiber	6.4 g
Protein	35.4 g
Sodium	322 mg

* Percent Daily Values are based on a 2,000 calorie diet.

MIE GORENG

(INDONESIAN FRIED NOODLES)

Ingredients

- 3 (3 ounce) packages ramen noodles (without flavor packets)
- 1 tbsp vegetable oil
- 1 pound skinless, boneless chicken breast halves, cut into strips
- 1 tsp olive oil
- 1 tsp garlic salt
- 1 pinch ground black pepper, or to taste
- 1 tbsp vegetable oil
- 1/2 cup chopped shallots
- 5 cloves garlic, chopped
- 1 cup shredded cabbage
- 1 cup shredded carrots
- 1 cup broccoli florets
- 1 cup sliced fresh mushrooms
- 1/4 cup soy sauce

- 1/4 cup sweet soy sauce (Indonesian <u>kecap manis</u>)
- 1/4 cup oyster sauce
- salt and pepper to taste

Directions

- Cook noodles in boiling water for about 3 minutes before running it through cold water to stop the process of cooking and draining all the water.
- Coat chicken strips with olive oil, black pepper and garlic salt before cooking it in hot oil for about 5 minutes or until you see that the chicken is no longer pink.
- Now add garlic and shallots, and cook them until you see that they are turning brown.
- Now add all the vegetables into the pan and cook it for another five minutes or until you see that the vegetables are tender.
- Add the mixture of noodles, soy sauce, oyster sauce and sweet soy sauce into the pan containing chicken and vegetables.
- Sprinkle some salt and pepper before serving.
- Enjoy.

Serving: 6

Timing Information:

Preparation	Cooking	Total Time
15 mins	25 mins	40 mins

Nutritional Information:

Calories	356 kcal
Carbohydrates	34 g
Cholesterol	43 mg
Fat	14.3 g
Fiber	1.7 g
Protein	22.7 g
Sodium	1824 mg

* Percent Daily Values are based on a 2,000 calorie diet.

PISANG GORENG

(INDONESIAN BANANA FRITTERS I)

Ingredients

- 1 1/4 cups all-purpose flour
- 2 tbsps granulated sugar
- 1/4 tbsp vanilla powder
- 1/2 cup milk
- 1 egg
- 2 tbsps butter, melted
- 1 tsp rum flavoring
- 4 ripe bananas, sliced
- 2 cups oil for frying

Directions

- Mix flour, vanilla powder and sugar before making a space in the center and adding milk, melted butter, egg and rum flavoring.

- Combine it thoroughly before adding banana slices.
- Fry this banana mixture in hot oil for about 15 minutes or until golden brown.
- Remove these bananas from the oil and drain it well with the help of paper towels.
- Serve.

Serving: 4

Timing Information:

Preparation	Cooking	Total Time
5 mins	15 mins	20 mins

Nutritional Information:

Calories	489 kcal
Carbohydrates	73.2 g
Cholesterol	64 mg
Fat	19.5 g
Fiber	5 g
Protein	8.3 g
Sodium	73 mg

* Percent Daily Values are based on a 2,000 calorie diet.

☐

KECAP MANIS SEDANG

(INDO-CHINESE SOY SAUCE)

Ingredients

- 2/3 cup soy sauce
- 1 cup water
- 2/3 cup brown sugar
- 8 bay leaves

Directions

- In a mixture of sugar, water and soy sauce in a saucepan, put bay leaves and bring all this to a boil.
- Now turn down the heat to medium and cook it for another 30 minutes.
- Let cool.

NOTE: This recipe is very important for multiple Indonesian and Indo-Chinese dishes mentioned throughout this cookbook.

Serving: 12

Timing Information:

Preparation	Cooking	Total Time
5 mins	15 mins	20 mins

Nutritional Information:

Calories	54 kcal
Carbohydrates	13.1 g
Cholesterol	0 mg
Fat	0 g
Fiber	0.1 g
Protein	0.9 g
Sodium	806 mg

* Percent Daily Values are based on a 2,000 calorie diet.

Satay Ayam

(Indo chicken with Peanut Sauce)

Ingredients

- 1 pound chicken thighs, cut into 1/2-inch pieces
- 3/4 tsp salt
- 1 pinch ground white pepper
- 1 tbsp sunflower seed oil
- 24 wooden skewers

Peanut Sauce:

- 1 cup water
- 5 tbsps peanut butter
- 2 tbsps kecap manis (sweet soy sauce)
- 1 tbsp brown sugar
- 2 cloves garlic, minced
- 1/2 tsp salt
- 1 tbsp lime juice

Directions

- Coat chicken thighs with ¾ tsp salt, sunflower seed oil and white pepper before refrigerating it for at least two hours.
- Bring a mixture of water, salt, peanut butter, <u>kecap manis</u>, garlic and brown sugar to boil before removing it from heat and adding some lime juice to make peanut sauce.
- Thread these chicken thighs onto skewers, while saving some marinade for later use.
- Cook these chicken thighs on a preheated grill for about 2 minutes each side or until tender.
- Serve this with peanut sauce.

NOTE: You can use a grilling plate as well for this recipe, just increase the cooking time of the meat. Use of a grill is preferred.

Serving: 4

Timing Information:

Preparation	Cooking	Total Time
10 mins	30 mins	40 mins

Nutritional Information:

Calories	326 kcal
Carbohydrates	8.9 g
Cholesterol	70 mg
Fat	21.8 g
Fiber	1.4 g
Protein	24.9 g
Sodium	1339 mg

* Percent Daily Values are based on a 2,000 calorie diet.

SKIRT STEAK

Ingredients

- 1 1/2 cups sweet soy sauce (Indonesian <u>kecap manis</u>)
- 1 cup sake
- 1 cup pineapple juice
- 1 cup mirin
- 1/2 cup reduced-sodium soy sauce
- 1/4 bunch fresh cilantro, chopped
- 1 tbsp white sugar
- 1 tbsp minced fresh ginger root
- 1 tbsp minced garlic
- 1 tbsp chopped scallions (green onions)
- 1 tbsp chili paste(optional)
- 1 (1 pound) skirt steak

Directions

- At first you need to set grill or grilling plate to medium heat and put some oil before starting anything else.

- Mix sweet soy sauce (kecap manis), scallions, sake, mirin, reduced-sodium soy sauce, cilantro, pineapple juice, sugar, ginger, garlic, and chili paste in large sized glass bowl before coating skirt steak with this mixture.
- Wrap it up with a plastic bag and marinate it for at least three hours.
- Remove every piece of meat from the marinade and cook this marinade in a saucepan for about 10 minutes over medium heat.
- Cook meat on the preheated grill for about 8 minutes each side or until tender.
- Serve it with the cooked marinade.

NOTE: If using a grilling plate please adjust the cooking time of the meat, to make sure that everything is cooked fully through.

Serving: 6

Timing Information:

Preparation	Cooking	Total Time
15 mins	20 mins	35 mins

Nutritional Information:

Calories	437 kcal
Carbohydrates	46.2 g
Cholesterol	27 mg
Fat	4.8 g
Fiber	1.4 g
Protein	22.5 g
Sodium	6517 mg

* Percent Daily Values are based on a 2,000 calorie diet.

Prawn Nasi Goreng

(Fried Rice and Shrimp In Sauce)

Ingredients

- 2 tbsps vegetable oil, divided
- 3 eggs, beaten
- 2 tbsps dark soy sauce
- 2 tbsps ketchup
- 1 tbsp brown sugar
- 1 tsp toasted sesame oil
- 1 tsp sweet chili sauce
- 1 zucchini, chopped
- 1 carrot, chopped
- 8 green onions, sliced
- 1 clove garlic, crushed
- 2 cups cooked rice
- 1/2 pound cooked prawns
- 2 tbsps fresh chives, chopped

Directions

- Cook egg in hot oil for about 30 seconds each side and cut it into smaller pieces after letting it cool down.
- Mix soy sauce, brown sugar, sesame oil, ketchup and chili sauce in a bowl, and set it aside for later use.
- Cook zucchini, green onions and carrot in hot oil for about three minutes before adding garlic, sauce mixture, rice and prawns.
- Turn the heat off and serve it by topping with eggs and sliced chives.

Serving: 2

Timing Information:

Preparation	Cooking	Total Time
20 mins	10 mins	30 mins

Nutritional Information:

Calories	664 kcal
Carbohydrates	67.7 g
Cholesterol	500 mg
Fat	25.5 g
Fiber	4 g
Protein	41 g
Sodium	1497 mg

* Percent Daily Values are based on a 2,000 calorie diet.

JEMPUT JUMPUT

(INDO BANANA FRITTERS II)

Ingredients

- 5/8 cup all-purpose flour
- 1 pinch salt
- 1 tsp baking powder
- 6 ripe bananas
- 3 tbsps white sugar
- oil for frying

Directions

- Add a mixture of baking powder, flour and salt slowly into mashed bananas and sugar, while stirring continuously.
- Drop this mixture with help of a spoon into hot oil and cook for about 8 minutes, while turning only once.
- Serve after draining with paper towels.

Serving: 18

Timing Information:

Preparation	Cooking	Total Time
10 mins	15 mins	25 mins

Nutritional Information:

Calories	491 kcal
Carbohydrates	14.4 g
Cholesterol	0 mg
Fat	49.1 g
Fiber	1.1 g
Protein	0.9 g
Sodium	49 mg

* Percent Daily Values are based on a 2,000 calorie diet.

CHICKEN & BROCCOLI

Ingredients

- 12 ounces boneless, skinless chicken breast halves, cut into bite-sized pieces
- 1 tbsp oyster sauce
- 2 tbsps dark soy sauce
- 3 tbsps vegetable oil
- 2 cloves garlic, chopped
- 1 large onion, cut into rings
- 1/2 cup water
- 1 tsp ground black pepper
- 1 tsp white sugar
- 1/2 medium head bok choy, chopped
- 1 small head broccoli, chopped
- 1 tbsp cornstarch, mixed with equal parts water

Directions

- Mix chicken, soy sauce and oyster sauce in large bowl and set it aside for later use.

- Cook garlic and onion in hot oil for about three minutes before adding chicken mixture and cooking it for another ten minutes.
- Now add water, sugar, broccoli, pepper and bok choy, and cook it for another ten minutes.
- In the end, add cornstarch mixture and cook it for another 5 minutes to get the sauce thick.
- Enjoy.

Serving: 6

Timing Information:

Preparation	Cooking	Total Time
10 mins	25 mins	35 mins

Nutritional Information:

Calories	170 kcal
Carbohydrates	9.8 g
Cholesterol	33 mg
Fat	7.9 g
Fiber	2.5 g
Protein	16.2 g
Sodium	418 mg

* Percent Daily Values are based on a 2,000 calorie diet.

☐

INDO-CHINESE SATE

(MEAT KABOBS)

Ingredients

- 1 onion, chopped
- 1 clove garlic, minced
- 1 1/2 tbsps kecap manis
- 1 tsp ground coriander
- 1 tsp ground cumin
- 1 tsp sambal oelek (sriracha sauce)
- 1/2 cup red wine
- 1 1/2 tbsps water
- 1 lemon grass, bruised, and cut into 1 inch pieces
- 1 pound sirloin steak, cut into 1-inch cubes

Directions

- At first you need to set a grill or grilling plate to medium heat and put some oil before starting anything else.

- Blend onion, garlic, coriander, cumin, <u>kecap manis</u>, sambal oelek, red wine and water in a blender until smooth before adding lemon grass and coating beef with this marinade.
- Wrap it up with a plastic bag and refrigerate it for at least two hours.
- Thread these beef pieces onto the skewers.
- Cook this on the preheated grill for about 5 minutes each side or until tender.

NOTE: If using a grilling plate please adjust the cooking time of the meat, to make sure that everything is cooked fully through.

Serving: 4

Timing Information:

Preparation	Cooking	Total Time
15 mins	5 mins	2 hr 20 mins

Nutritional Information:

Calories	200 kcal
Carbohydrates	6.5 g
Cholesterol	69 mg
Fat	5.4 g
Fiber	0.9 g
Protein	25.1 g
Sodium	419 mg

* Percent Daily Values are based on a 2,000 calorie diet.

TELUR BALADO

(SPICY INDONESIAN EGGS)

Ingredients

- 1 cup vegetable oil for frying
- 6 hard-boiled eggs, shells removed
- 6 red chili peppers, seeded and chopped
- 4 cloves garlic
- 4 medium shallots
- 2 tomatoes, quartered
- 1 tsp shrimp paste
- 1 1/2 tbsps peanut oil
- 1 tbsp vegetable oil
- 1 tsp white vinegar
- 1 tsp white sugar
- salt and pepper to taste

Directions

- Deep fry eggs in a pan for about seven minutes over medium heat or until golden brown in color.

- Put chili peppers, shallots, garlic, tomatoes, and shrimp in a blender until you see that the required smoothness is achieved.
- Cook chili pepper mixture in hot oil before adding vinegar, pepper, sugar, fried eggs and salt into a mixture.
- Turn down the heat to medium and cook it for about 5 minutes, while turning it frequently.
- Serve.

Serving: 6

Timing Information:

Preparation	Cooking	Total Time
15 mins	20 mins	35 mins

Nutritional Information:

Calories	237 kcal
Carbohydrates	13.1 g
Cholesterol	201 mg
Fat	17.3 g
Fiber	1.4 g
Protein	9.1 g
Sodium	115 mg

* Percent Daily Values are based on a 2,000 calorie diet.

Ayam Masak Merah

(Spicy Tomato Chicken)

Ingredients

- 1 (3 pound) whole chicken, cut into 8 pieces
- 1 tsp ground turmeric
- salt to taste
- 1/4 cup dried red chili peppers
- 3 fresh red chili pepper, finely chopped
- 4 cloves garlic, minced
- 1 red onion, chopped
- 1 (3/4 inch thick) slice fresh ginger root
- 2 tbsps sunflower seed oil
- 1 cinnamon stick
- 2 whole star anise pods
- 5 whole cloves
- 5 cardamom seeds
- 2 tomatoes, sliced
- 2 tbsps ketchup
- 1 tsp white sugar, or to taste

- 1/2 cup water
-

Directions

- Coat chicken with turmeric powder and salt, and set it aside for later use.
- Put dried red chili peppers in hot water until you see that it is soft.
- Put softened dried chili, garlic, fresh red chili peppers, onion, and ginger in a blender and blend it until you get a paste.
- Cook chicken in hot oil until you see that it is golden from all sides and set it aside.
- Now cook chili paste, cinnamon, cardamom seeds, star anise, and cloves in the same pan for few minutes before adding chicken and water into it.
- Add tomatoes, sugar and ketchup, and bring all this to a boil before turning down the heat to medium and cooking for another 15 minutes.

- Serve.

Serving: 4

Timing Information:

Preparation	Cooking	Total Time
20 mins	35 mins	55 mins

Nutritional Information:

Calories	462 kcal
Carbohydrates	15.4 g
Cholesterol	92 mg
Fat	29.7 g
Fiber	3.3 g
Protein	33.6 g
Sodium	183 mg

* Percent Daily Values are based on a 2,000 calorie diet.

CAP CAI

(INDO-CHINESE SHRIMP VEGGIE SALAD)

Ingredients

- 3 tbsps vegetable oil
- 4 cloves garlic, minced
- 1 onion, thinly sliced
- 10 ounces peeled and deveined medium shrimp (30-40 per pound)
- 1 head bok choy, chopped
- 1 1/2 cups chopped broccoli
- 1 1/2 cups chopped cauliflower
- 1 large carrot, thinly sliced at an angle
- 3 green onions, chopped
- 2/3 cup water
- 2 tbsps cornstarch
- 2 tbsps fish sauce
- 2 tbsps oyster sauce
- 1 tsp white sugar

- 1/2 tsp ground black pepper
- salt to taste

Directions

- Cook onion and garlic in hot oil for about five minutes before adding shrimp, broccoli, cauliflower, bok choy, carrot, water and green onion, and cook this for about 15 minutes or until you see that all the vegetables are tender.
- Add a mixture of fish sauce and cornstarch, to the cap cai and also some oyster sauce, pepper and sugar.
- Mix it thoroughly and add some salt according to your taste before serving.

Serving: 4

Timing Information:

Preparation	Cooking	Total Time
20 mins	25 mins	45 mins

Nutritional Information:

Calories	250 kcal
Carbohydrates	18.7 g
Cholesterol	106 mg
Fat	11.9 g
Fiber	4.4 g
Protein	18.9 g
Sodium	819 mg

* Percent Daily Values are based on a 2,000 calorie diet.

A Southeast Asian Sandwich

Ingredients

- 4 boneless pork loin chops, cut 1/4 inch thick
- 4 (7 inch) French bread baguettes, split lengthwise
- 4 tsps mayonnaise, or to taste
- 1 ounce chile sauce with garlic (sriracha sauce)
- 1/4 cup fresh lime juice
- 1 small red onion, sliced into rings
- 1 medium cucumber, peeled and sliced lengthwise
- 2 tbsps chopped fresh cilantro
- salt and pepper to taste

Directions

- Put pork chops in a broiling pan and cook it for about 5 minutes or until you see that it is brown from each side.

- Put mayonnaise evenly on French rolls and also put one pork chop on each roll.
- Put chili sauce on the meat and add some lime juice, while topping it with onion, pepper, cucumber, salt and cilantro.
- Add some more lime juice just before serving.

Serving: 4

Timing Information:

Preparation	Cooking	Total Time
10 mins	5 mins	15 mins

Nutritional Information:

Calories	627 kcal
Carbohydrates	72.1 g
Cholesterol	124 mg
Fat	12.1 g
Fiber	3.3 g
Protein	55.3 g
Sodium	1005 mg

* Percent Daily Values are based on a 2,000 calorie diet.

A GIFT FROM ME TO YOU...

I know you like cultural food. But what about Japanese Sushi?

Join my private mailing list of readers and get a copy of *Infinite Sushi: A*

Complete Set of Sushi and Japanese Recipes by fellow BookSumo author Hashimoto Kazuma for FREE!

Sign Me Up!

Enjoy some of the best sushi available!

You will also receive updates about all my new books when they are free. So please show your support.

Also don't forget to like and subscribe on the social networks. I love meeting my readers. Links to all my profiles are below so please click and connect :)

Facebook

Twitter

COME ON...
LET'S BE FRIENDS :)

I adore my readers and love connecting with them socially. Please follow the links below so we can connect on Facebook, Twitter, and Google+.

Facebook

Twitter

I also have a blog that I regularly update for my readers so check it out below.

My Blog

Can I Ask A Favour?

If you found this book interesting, or have otherwise found any benefit in it. Then may I ask that you post a review of it on Amazon? Nothing excites me more than new reviews, especially reviews which suggest new topics for writing. I do read all reviews and I always factor feedback into my newer works.

So if you are willing to take ten minutes to write what you sincerely thought about this book then please visit our Amazon page and post your opinions.

Again thank you!

INTERESTED IN OTHER EASY COOKBOOKS?

Everything is easy check out some of my other cookbooks:

Grilling:

Easy Grilling Cookbook

Smoothies:

Easy Smoothie Cookbook

Nutella

Easy Nutella Cookbook

Korean Cuisine:

Easy Korean Cookbook

Filipino Cuisine:

Easy Filipino Cookbook

Quiche:

Easy Quiche Cookbook

Burgers:

Easy Burger Cookbook

Cupcakes:

Easy Cupcake Cookbook

Mexican Cuisine:

Easy Mexican Cookbook

Dumplings:

Easy Dumpling Cookbook

Doughnuts:

Easy Doughnut Cookbook

Thai Cuisine:

Easy Thai Cookbook

Made in the USA
Las Vegas, NV
06 July 2021